PORTRAIT OF A YOUNG MAN

PORTRAIT OF

A YOUNG MAN:

POEMS

OLIVER BARNES

WITH LESSONS

FROM HIS TEACHER

2022-2025

DUTCH POET PRESS

ISBN Number 979-8-9929264-2-2

DUTCH POET PRESS

Palo Alto, California
dutcpoetpress.com
rhperry51@gmail.com

Cover and Interior Images:
Untitled by Oliver Barnes
Watercolor Collage, 2020

To Teachers and Students
Everywhere

FOREWORD

Lessons from his teacher

Beginning in fall 2022, I began to give poetry lessons to Oliver Barnes. I'm grateful for this fabulous gift along with the interest and suppport of his parents who made this book possible.

I've found this assignment to be a wonderful opportunity to share the world of poetry and publishing, history and translation, art and design with a young student of remarkable talent and curiosity.

In our weekly sessions, I enjoyed introducing Oliver to poetry from around the world, including his own traditions both East and West. For example, he has become acquainted wth the ancient Chinese literati who practiced what is called the Three Perfections—poetry, painting, and calligraphy.

He has also been learning about the creative process and endeavors integral to the art of poetry such as book design and publishing, editing and translation, while responding to myriad sources of inspiration from nature and culture, history and philosophy, mythology and religion/spirituality.

Our weekly sessions have developed into an extraordinary learning experience of exchange and collaboration for teacher and student alike.

— *Robert Perry*

POEMS

CUP BY CUP

Draining water
from a pool
while using
a cup, it has been
hours but
it is something to do
so I say why not!

DAY IN THE LIFE: JOURNEY POEM

Where waves meet the sky
turning a bright yellow ...

in the joy of reading
writing and learning
still half asleep
lumbering out of bed
waiting for the sun's gift
the day will bring
bestowing his splendor
on his subjects

Where water meets land
a jagged gray of stone ...

climbing up a ridge
to a view of mountains
tough stone can pierce
the skin handholds make
rocks crumble as I ascend
the mighty rays of the sun
scorch the land
sweat dripping down
but I persist

Where mountain meets fog
murky white with drops ...

rushing home at dusk
when the birds fly swiftly
flapping their delicate wings
like glass that cannot be broken

the dusk extinguishing
the light of day slowly
darkness rising covering
the earth until it falls asleep
under the moon and stars

DEER PARK
After Wang Wei

Looking through empty branches
    dead silence scattered round the mountain

Yet from the distance I catch
    the presence of human words and laughter

Thin threads of light
    coursing through a cacophony of leaves

Weaving through darkness
    green moss illuminated above

FOG

Misty white waves
not of ocean
but
of fog rolling
over the mountain

Blocks the sun
saps the warmth
but yet

sooths
the animals

Silence is
crouches
as the mist
climbs the
mountain

FOUR SEASONS

Summer
Running down the gravel
Sweat trickling down

Autumn
Rain splattering
Socks soaked

Winter
White dots fall
Barren ground
Tundra by the second

Spring
Birds chirping merrily
Grass pokes at my feet

HAIKU

eyelids blink open
pillow underneath my head
calls for breakfast ring

raindrops falling
eyes to the ground

splash in
start kicking
gulp in air

LEAVES OF GRASS #1
[Song of Myself]

After Walt Whitman

I celebrate myself,
for today is a perfect day
to exist.

The dawn is waking
the animals are chirping
cawing,
clawing,
and singing

Everything is not perfect
yet it is in its own way.

The sounds of cars passing by
make the city alive,
and as the city's
buildings shine to
life, the city comes
to life.

A new day to
start a new song.

LEAVES OF GRASS #2
[Song of Myself]

After Walt Whitman

I celebrate myself,
singing with the birds to
all men and women alike
the dead and the living
for as the generous pleasures of life

to the blades of grass enduring
the winter cold and yet accept death
and find peace in the icy frost
feeding on the wet of autumn

to the dying and the sick
still hoping against hope

that there might be one
day that they will be
able to sing among
the birds, grass, trees
and the living, all alike

to the workers in coal mines,
toiling about for hours
under the icy embrace of winter
still singing among themselves
singing about happiness,
singing about
hope

LOST AND FOUND

Standing at the gates
I tremble
leaving the familiar behind
walking into a new beginning

I step into a future unknown
shining with possibilities
a new sun offering me
a new life

Filling my heart
with the joys of learning
filling the school
with new friendships
finding others
who share my interests

And still a tear is shed from my eye
still a sorrow lies still in my soul
There are the memories
          of friends I knew before
they resound in me
                on an autumn day

And yet I smile at the rustling wind
through the leaves

LUCHTFIETSER (Daydreamer)

Staring into the sky
unfocusing eyes
mind thinking about things to think

Stuck in this room
bland white walls
I am a bird trapped in a cage

Months and months like this
missing Spring and its warmth
I ask myself: What will I do
when I'm free…

GLISTENING LIGHT
After William Carlos Williams

so much depends
upon

a glistening
light

below the dark
roof

covered in
a dusty mist

NIGHT HOUSE

Creeping down the shadowcast stairs
    alone

I see the painting on the wall
    hard black stones

The window opens onto a starry night
    small shining dots
    in an ocean of inky darkness

**TAO
TE
CHING:
NINE**

Milk the cow a pail too many
it will kick the pail over

Spank the child for the wrongdoing
the lesson will not be learned

When the work has already been done,
why do more?

NOTHING INTO WHITE
After Han Kang

When thinking about
everything
dissolving
my thoughts
into
nothing—
that infinite always

A strange absence
calling up the pure
essence of nothing
wondering
how have I captured
that no-thing-ness

I saw its true face and form
in the darkness revealing
the cold, soft face
of death

And yet when we are
young and disregardful
of death we realize that
emptiness could never
mask the irrevocable
presence of white

GRAVITY

Exempt from
everything
but this

By the will
of nature
I am bound
to fall

I keep your
namesake
in my part
to wonder

Teach me
to fish
and I'll fish
for the rest
of my life

Give me
the ground
to walk on
free to live
my life

I'll
remember
your name
and the
miracle that
saved me

UNREQUITED LOVE
After Charles Simic

Nearing dusk
when he finds the
hiding place of countless trinkets
guided by half-light
he sees
a matchbox adorned
with instrumental verse
a velvet doll shrouded
in metal wire
eyes following
him in a trance-like
stare

Clear they had not
been touched
meant for another era
a grander age

better to yield less wear
untouched and precious
forsaken than spoiled
in ruins

He glances at his watch
nine-thirty
without another look
he leaves the room
relics of the past
    enduring their
        solitude

UNTITLED (Human Acts)
After Han Kang

unlikely undisturbed
tonight
shadows linger
on the faces of
the dead

once the rites
begin
cold frail
cries heard
resonating
against
the pale air

half
formal
lights from
the city are
dead

tonight
the moths share
a room with the
assurance of quiet

from the day
they swore
to know nothing
but love

to the night
spent with tears shed

cold hearts swallow
bodies to pieces
too numb to share

Ere long
the sun shall rise

vanquish
the rising fog

THE MOON CAN'T REMEMBER ANYTHING
After Li Young-Li

You were watching
when I fell into the water
gasping for breath
reaching into
the sky

You dragged me
ashore where the sand
pierced my flesh
the wind cut me open
freeing my spirit

The rain washed
away my tears of
unbound sorrows
flooding the Earth

My will now clarified
my soul bound
to survive
in your presence

THIRTEEN WAYS OF LOOKING AT A DEER
After Wallace Stevens

I
At the break of dawn
the deer skips into the clearing
beckoning the world to awaken

II
My two eyes dart across the room
of a jungle
like a pair of deer
looking for ten bloodthirsty lions

III
Art is a matter of life and death
the deer living the life of the artist

IV
Rainwater falls on the deer
washing away her grief
  counting the tears
one after the other

V
I believe in miracles
when I am profounded
at how the deer softly grooms
the afternoon sun in her wake

VI
These misty forests
their arms stripped of leaves
the deer's fur is
mistaken for cedar skin
with shadows staring

VII
O you who fear
those from other worlds
Do you not notice how the
mountain trembles?
At the mere sight of the deer's
paralyzing gaze?

VII
I know graceful melodies
dancing about the ears of the crowd
But I know, too,
that the deer's harmonious singing is involved
in what I know

IX
When the deer galloped out of sight,
an emptiness filled the forest
where I discovered her absence

X
Into the lighting set up for dawn,
the deer blantantly trods out
Never have these colors
appeared so vividly or coarse

XI
He skipped along
the rolling hills
Frozen with alarm
he mistook the rhythm
of his stride for the deer

XII
The entire village is conversing
the deer must be staring

XIII
It was evening all afternoon
The light busy burying itself
among the trees where the deer
prepares herself for sleep
Do you not notice how the
mountain trembles?
At the mere sight of the deer's
paralyzing gaze?

DREAM

Your shine outdone
only by the moonlight

Grace carried me weightless
and silent though I heard
a whistling wind

Fur dappled milky white
eyes ablaze
suspicion in your
pupils turned to gaze
at me in a stare

I couldn't help
but watch you
striding toward me

Was it my frightened look?

ON TURNING TEN
After Billy Collins

A toy car, a gift from a friend
now sitting in a dark garage
The blaring siren of a truck horn
no longer startles me

I used to run around the house
screaming with joy

Now I lay on my bed
staring blankly at the ceiling

Writing poetry
I relive my experiences
letting my imagination get
the better of me
gasping for breath, flailing
my arms about
trying to keep from sinking
into the murky abyss
swallowing me whole

Growing older it seems
the spark of creativity once free
is now bound to my aging self
clawing my way out
of the abyss
turning it into a vast world
waiting to be explored

I stare out the window
watching the younger kids
in the neighborhood
playing ball
I decide to join them

I AM

I am from Instant Raman, half-eaten steak
and broken shoes

I am from the Harry Potter book on the shelf
unread and unnoticed

I am from the basil plant buried in the dirt
the orange tree in my backyard
the oranges never tasted sweet enough

I am from white moon cakes and determination
from Elana and William

I am from ambition and hard-working
and kindness

I am from a promise and dumplings

I am from California and China
rice and pork

I am from the time my mother built
a telescope from the picture-book
on the counter

PROSE POEM: A CHILD'S CHRISTMAS
After Dylan Thomas

When the snow fell in white sheets almost like a
blanket, I looked out the half-covered window and
told my friend about the things we could do
with the soft snow.

"We should build a snowman."

"No, we should dig out paths."

He slowly opened the door … Creeeaaak! … Rushing
out, he grabbed a shovel and started digging. I chuckled.
He was doing all the work, while I sat down and read a
book beside the fire.

Eventually, I joined the fray, to feel the joy of purpose.

NIGHT SKY

Branches peeled back
for a gateway
to the night sky
the moon softly illuminated
hangs like a spotlight
over the clouds
—prelude
to the stars

SUMMER EVENING

The heat of the wrathful
summer leaves with the night

Constellations
held behind
clouds of silvery red
stars wait
for their moment
to shine

I walk through
the fluttering expanse
of crimson
caught in a world
of half dreams

I take solace
in the glory
which once was
as the dark enters
and the crickets
begin to stir

INVISIBLE

Shadows seep back into
my world
I find myself
invisible
rejoicing in the
darkness

the night wind
dancing in my ear
whispering secrets
I never before
could understand

I reply by
pouring out
my secrets
waiting
all too long
to be released

shackles lifted at last
my destiny to discover
myself looking at myself
disappearing
with my sorrows
before the day
returns

CUP BY CUP

Draining water
from a pool
while using
a cup, it has been
hours but
it is something to do
so I say why not!

Wrinkles form
my back aches
like it's on fire
but it is something
to do so I say why not!

Like a worker
cutting grass
with a knife refuses
a mower
he's exhausted
but it is something to do
so he says
why not!

NOTES

The primary purpose of this collection of poems is education and enrichment with a shared dedication and delight in learning the art of poetry transacted through an exchange of teacher and student. These are the resources that contributed to and benefited what Oliver learned and the marvelous poems he wrote.

Day in the Life: Journey Poem (Page 3)
For this poem, Oliver was introduced to the "Three Perfections: Painting, Poetry and Calligraphy," a hallmark of the Chinese Literati tradition, with the help of the book *Three Perfections: Chinese Painting, Poetry and Calligraphy* by art historian Michael Sullivan (Thames and Hudson, 1974). Oliver was also informed by a journey poem in three sections written by his teacher called "Along the Border of Heaven" inspired by the book *Along the Border of Heaven: Yuan and Sung Paintings from the C. C. Wang Collection* by Richard Barnhart (Metropolitan Museum of Art, 1983). The multi-page frontispiece of the hardcover edition features an ink painting of a river journey titled *Cloud Mountains* (c1365) by Fung Ts'ung-i with a poem by Li Po (701-762 CE) provided by the book's author. Li Po's poem concludes with the resonant words "Flowing along the border of heaven."

Deer Park (Page 4)
His poem is drawn from the book *19 Ways of Looking at Wang Wei: With More Ways* by Eliot Weinberger (New Directions, 2016), a study of a prominent poem "Deer Park" by the T'ang dynasty literati figure in translation. Robert chose Gary Snyder's translation from which Oliver was asked to provide his rendition of the Wang Wei poem based on how Snyder rendered it. Student and teacher, and the editor Weinberger, agree this rendering was among the most evocative in the book. the poem references the Deer Park at Sarnath in India where the Buddha taught.

Leaves of Grass #1 and #2 (Pages 8-9)
After *Leaves of Grass: The First (1855) Edition*. Penguin Classics, 1961.

Glistening Light (Page 12)
After "The Red Wheelbarrow" by William Carlos Williams from *poets.org*, website of the American Academy of Poets.

Tao Te Ching: Nine (Page 14)
after the *Tao Te Ching* by Lao Tzu. Harper Perennial Modern Classics, 2006. Translation by Stephen Mitchell.

Nothing into White (Page 15)
After *The White Book* by Han Kang. Hogarth Press, 2017. Translation by Deborah Smith. In addition to the book, Robert shared and discussed with Oliver an interview the 2024 Nobel Laureate Han Kang gave about her life as a writer (Louisiana Museum of Art in Denmark, 2019).

Unrequited Love (Page 17)
After poems by Charles Simic on artist Joseph Cornell from *Dime-Store Alchemy* by Charles Simic. New York Review of Books Classics, 2006.

Untitled (Human Acts) (Page 18)
After *Human Acts* by Han Kang. Hogarth Press, 2017. Translation by Deborah Smith. Also informed by the interview with Han Kang mentioned above.

The Moon Can't Remember Anything (Page 19)
After "The Moon Can't Remember Anything" by Li Young-Li from *poets.org*, website of the American Academy of Poets.

Thirteen Ways of Looking at a Deer (Pages 20-22)
After "Thirteen Ways of Looking at a Blackbird" by Wallace Stevens from *The Collected Poems of Wallace Stevens*. Vintage, 2015. Oliver paid close attention to the distinctive ways Stevens wrote each section, which

Oliver strove to replicate in his own observations of the animal he chose to write about. This was a rigorous lesson from a master poet of applied technique of his craft.

On Turning Ten (Page 24)
After having actually just turned 10 years old himself, Oliver provided his take on the experience after reading "On Turning Ten" by Billy Collins from *The Art of Drowning*. University of Pittsburgh Press, 1995.

Prose Poem: A Child's Christmas (Page 26)
After "A Child's Christmas in Wales" by Dylan Thomas from A New Directions Book with woodcuts by Ellen Raskin, New York, 2003 (previously 1954 and 1959).

CONTENTS

COLOPHON

Cover & Interior Design – Robert Perry, Dutch Poet Press
Typefaces – PMN Caecilia Sans, Fletcher Typewriter
Printing | Distribution – IngramSpark